MW00508899

Dead Relics

Leon J. Gratton

Grosvenor House
Publishing Limited

All rights reserved
Copyright © Leon J. Gratton, 2022

The right of Leon J. Gratton to be identified as the author of this
work has been asserted in accordance with Section 78
of the Copyright, Designs and Patents Act 1988

The book cover is copyright to Leon J. Gratton

This book is published by
Grosvenor House Publishing Ltd
Link House
140 The Broadway, Tolworth, Surrey, KT6 7HT.
www.grosvenorhousepublishing.co.uk

This book is sold subject to the conditions that it shall not, by way of
trade or otherwise, be lent, resold, hired out or otherwise circulated
without the author's or publisher's prior consent in any form of binding or
cover other than that in which it is published and
without a similar condition including this condition being imposed
on the subsequent purchaser.

A CIP record for this book
is available from the British Library

ISBN 978-1-80381-347-9

Content

FOREWORD

This book of poetry is inspired by all the girls who have loved me, came through my life, broke my heart, taught right from wrong and basically been there from the early days of my childhood to my age now, especially the likes of Dawn who inspired a lot of my later work (By the way the poems aren't in order). But if she can't figure out which are for her then she'd be as well giving up all hope in reading poetry of a symbolic nature and true love put through it. As well as the many women who have inspired this poetry there are political influences and environmental struggles. Then there are the ghosts of old heroes like JIM MORRISON, HENDRIX, BOB DYLAN and PINK FLOYD. This book, if you don't mind my egocentric rant here, is totally amazing and worth a read for anyone who likes dead relics and things that never age. Maybe I'm hoping too much but I hope you enjoy the reading of this book and don't take the blood stains seriously they belong to me.

DEAD RELICS

Soothe the ways of dead relics
Come quietly to the ways of dead relics
Please be my giver easier, pleaser of dead relics
Hellish in politics with wasting of dead relics
Death of the scream yet to dream of dead relics
Quietly obscene on the scene of dead relics
Dead relics are the names of those we forgive
In absurdity, and murder, bye to those dead relics

IN A POOL OF
ANGELIC TEARS

If I drown my sorrows
In a pool of Angelic tears
Will you know of tomorrow
Will you share my fears
If I go down to Devils
You know the addiction of trust
Forget the heavens
As it becomes sport like in lust
They say the world turns that way
But summoning ancients
To be my girl
Will only show me I'm a slave
Psychotic trances
With pressure and stress
Puppets dancing
Whilst I try to look my best
Are we that vain
And Shallow
With all the pain
And sorrow
Is it for you I wander
This misery and shame
Will it tear me asunder
To an open dirt like grave

I know lust
I know trust
I know love
I've seen it move with the setting sun
The stars in the evening
The clouds the moon
You saw me leaving
But did you summon a tomb
My words on the shelf
All gathering dust
They say I'm petty
Cause I no longer trust
The poetic mind is one of confusion
The poetic mind is one of delusion
Artistic temperament is what I have
If you only knew me
You would be glad
So I say I'll drown myself
In Angelic tears
With words to myself
No more my fears
If you hold on too tight
Love will slip away
But if you kick and fight
It will darken your day
Now the clouds that cover
My very stars
Shall soothe a purple soul
And cover my scars
The rumble of hunger
In a midnight mist
Shall quiet the thunder
With lovers twists

CIRCLES IN THE SAND

The time is at hand
   With circles in the sand
The love I had so dear
Is relative to fear
I cross those lines
And love is so blind
It was small and broken
The world I lived in
With no words spoken
I think I can love again
Without the aggravation
Without the pain
Some live in hope
Of a clean-like soak
In the winter rain
Where the heartache is gone
For worlds of sullen pain
I close my eyes
To the blue like mists
I mustn't be hasty
As I know love exists
She shined a smile a quick hello
But it's taken so long

I'm afraid I must go
To the purple midnight
That heavenly delight
There are two I love
And the appearance of a dove
Show peace that is in sight
My god, protector and holder
Of the heavenly light
She has a radiant way
With would turn the head of any Christian slave

PEACEFUL MOONS

The feeling, the thoughts
   The lust and love it brought
It's silent with humour
And a passionate glance
Like peaceful moons
I may take a chance
Her eyes of blue
Her long dark hair
I'll see her soon
Tho' all I do is stare
If she'll be my muse
And lover
And excuse

QUIET ONES

I am caught with fire in my soul
I am gradually losing control
Love songs of girls with hearts on fire
Love songs with souls on fire
Souls singing in Angelic choirs
Souls fulfilling heavenly desires
Apollo wondrous now an Idol no longer a god
The Pain of the stars in sullen watchful gaze
A wondrous valley, a wondrous place
With women in the light, and shadows missing in the
sun
It's beauty in wonder we become
Light beams and quiet ones

DREAMS SUDDENLY ARISING

Dreams suddenly arising
Breaking the night with spider web cracks
The gold ness of the sun holding our lives
With edges and clouds and pin point accuracy
It's running with a horse that shows
The finality of the worlds course
Glad you are for these dreams
Even tho' we are littered with brain disease

ANGELIC

B e a giver of hope
In a worldly trance

Be my lover of life
So that we may dance

Be my honey dewed princess
In this warm house of Jade

Be my lover of mercy
Yet never fade

Be my sweet and kindness
And wondrous Temptress

Be my sullen sad highness
And never my damsel in distress

Be my quiet gentle wonder
And angelic like lover

GHOSTS BECOME GODS

True ways of the sublime
True the Venus of time
True the closeness of rhyme
I watch with the heart of an angel
He turns to the crossroads and finds the devil
That two faced Joker who lives in the soul of ghosts
My personality torn in two
What's in the soul of a drug addict
Cold swollen brew
My heart fractured in this cold rest
This town superstitious to the unfamiliar rest
People try to help but I've been cursed
To win my soul back, what could be worse
Love is stronger than evil. I hope is what they say
Quiet cruel words in the mind in the way
People of the valley will become strong
And arise from the shadows to right their wrongs
Ghosts being bettered
By sullen golden words
Crisp in the summer
Whilst the swallow becomes a lord
It's fateful in scrutiny
That ghosts become words
With times impurities
That ghosts become gods

HANGMAN'S ROPE

Time oh sweet time
It raises eyebrows
In the infants mind
We become sad yet happy
Reaching for stars
It's with love and trust
We live in hope
Dawning hour
The hangman's rope
Quiet we become
Whilst shadows darken our door
I open my wings, and floating I soar
Just off the ground
Moving fast away from the crowd
These things seem impossible
But the Azure shroud
Has become the lords language
And with this I'm proud
In ancient test
Lust and sex
Are forbidden
But tears in my eyes
See through the lies
And show that love
Is in our very lives

And angelic hours
Turn away from unholy towers
Ones that show the rats
The slaves
Whilst families pay not
For unearthly graves
Hoping to become a star filled son
With dawning slaves
I become
Another one, in the sun
Blind to the point
With my life and soul saved
If love is so true
Then why so black
And why so blue
Quiet now hush
Quiet now please
As I've been through so much
My words sleep with ease

THORNS AND SCARS

The honesty of religion
Takes us away from oblivion
Christ-like with thorns and scars
Pushing to limits we get closer to stars
The angelic lives we lead
In the winters cold moon
With people going on their way
The season has come too soon
But embrace to take away psychological scars
It must be heavenly going to the sun
Where we drown our melancholy
With Fun! Fun! Fun!

TRUE

Cast not an eye in sin
For sin and redemption
Turn into the eye
And become thys enemy
With heavenly abodes you must
Win the heart of true love
And cast off pale shallow trust
And hold those dear to you close
With mind like fury neither scorn or strike in anger
But with tenderness hold a thought on temperate love
Then doubt not the fuelling comfort of a girls warmth

DEATH OF SOLDIERS

The moon chasing stars
Silver tipped with chaotic mars
The turning of the world
Goodbye sweetness
Goodbye wondrous girl
I'm sorry for the words of spite
I'd rather live in wondrous night
You say none neither
With words of serenity
Whilst sleaze does but slither
And gone is my sin
Gone rotten cold weather
Come please, be my giver
Fractured heart with dying liver
My death shall come happy to some
But kisses and buss
Of true gentleness
Shall quiet the rotten beggars vile slow tongue
That begins to seep lies and turn on some
While money breads disease and some
Wish for it just to please
But angels are brought
I said brought not bought
All the money on the wealth of giants shoulders
I've said it many a time I'd rather not feel
Than be the death of soldiers

SILVER NIGHT

Which with time
   Silver night
Golden dawn
On the mind
Quickness comes
To sullen sombre rest
And beginnings of life
Will show our best
Artistic in showings
Gone to our strife
Never in death
Yet never slowing
With each and every breath
My mind starts showing
Worlds in which we left
The sun ever glowing

ANGELIC FLOWER

I awoke to the singing of a precious maid
Revived I listened and was at total peace
I could smell the honey of our night of passion
Ambrosia to my senses the girl a goddess
The more I think on it the more is the hour
With honey dewed princess with angelic flower
Jealous I am of such passion of late
Yet I do not know who she is and the
Arrow is straight

DRAGONS FLOWER

The dragons flower
  Protected by the highest tower
The princess Gold standing in
Seas and rivers of bluest blue
The shoulders of giants
Which we worship the holy planets
Infernos abyss who only gods
May steal their kiss
With the ancient plough we create
Worlds and universes
A world of immortals which is what we are
We forgot days in which we shopped in the
Bizarre
The ancient magic which binds
This world gives us belief on a living world
Curses of old which are bound onto me
Show the heavens are yet too open for you and me
I see my life through a scrying eye
Such wonder and beauty for you and I
Blessings come with the summer shower
And I turn it into a ring
The Dragons flower

EARTH'S SHALLOW GRAVE

It's quiet out there
I return the stare
Victimless no one is
Even though dragons
Become golden fish
I hear the moan again and again
Hoping that this world will someday
Find an empty grave
The midnight lovers
Who have no right
Rape is what they summoned
Not daylight
Cruel to be kind aint no ancient way
I'd rather shed my blood on
Earths shallow grave

DECEIVED

Living is tough
But sure enough
It's a quote in a book
Some say god is dead
But look me in the eye
And read through what I've said
If god is dead
Then why do we dangle on
Deaths thread
We must endure something's
This I believe
But God dying
You have been deceived!!!!

OPEN THE WOUND

Go with stars and tear open the wound
Heartfelt I wonder if with Angels
Applauding us
My dreams come too soon
It's love and feelings which become
Sore in my heart
The broken promise and love to start
Fortune seen, living in this world
Of confusion
I love too much but call it not an
Intrusion

THE FIRST PLAY

The world slowly shows us reverence
In the first play
Love is but nought and doubt
In the first play
Feelings they have none, cold and strange
In the first play
Wonder if Nietzsche knows of wounds
In the first play
Poetic and prose laying into my heart
In the first play
Gone is her laughter, now she but cries
In the first play
Find them feel them gone
In the first play
True love she doesn't know it
In the first play
If she did she wouldn't have teased me
In the first play

OCEANS OF TIME

The world dawning with golden sun
You pair of goddesses
But who has time for love
As thoughtful as it might be
I cannot come across your vast less seas
Oceans of time
In star filled night
Heavenly in its existence
And vast in its delight
You wondrous Goddesses
I hear you every might
I feel your radiance
Your unknown
And out of sight

SPICE

In thoughts of cold winter love
I'll wait here whilst she has fun
Gone quiet I become a poet
She always says goodbye
And some nights oh so lonely I cry
Wondering whether our love exists
An exotic time a wondrous bliss
I live quiet in those eyes
That burn with fire and show me skies
It's Dawn chasing the night away
But I'm afraid of her wrath
She doesn't need to tell me twice
As her sugar and love come to me
Like an opiate type spice

POLICE

Quiet it is in this room
Where the buzz of confusion leaves us too soon
The Sunday summer, shimmering haze
Leaves with resolution leaves those days
Hendrix plays in the background the bar is closed
No more the stone, No more the buzz
I wonder who called them in
Was it them or us

NUMB BRAIN

I call to you silently with mind and heart
Of will
It's easy to disguise
It's easy to thrill
With a chance to be a king in this glorious world
With music that makes me smile
Sullen the song waits and makes me weep
Quiet the child his is about sombre sleep
The night in quiet peaceful times
Numb brain
No rain
Oh what a surprise

PASSIONS HOURS

The cold horrific glory
   With gold on summers horizon
She plays with my mind
A summoner of winds
With a temperate thief
The poison of an assassin
Unknown the relief
To unreasonable love
A grave stone and savage marble
Cant they leave him alone
In his glory and pardon

I move with cunning
To the woman of dark hair
She acts so cold as tho' she doesn't care
But play on this game of skill
It's not so sudden
It's not about a thrill
With grave yards yawning
And night gently crawling
Past these pitch black hours
Princess of gold
Will live in Passions hours

CREATURES

Being of starlight matter
Creatures die every day
And leave those to become
The earth bound slave
With wisdom looking on with her owl
Those with troubles should hear the moon howl

PROSIAC SLAVES

I'm out there again
In glory in pain
Of love lost gone to intrusion
I'm left with this deadly confusion
In ignorance the poetic way
The sullen time is on it's way
To become a lover
Of nights only way
To become another
Of words endless ways
To be a lover
Of prosaic slaves
Hopefully you'll read this
And come away thinking
That the summers sun is ray like in hope

POETIC WAR

We live in the poetic war
   Slow and decisively I take a draw
On a sunlit, Sparklike, Cigarette
The saviour coming in books of infinite time
We read on in the wise ancient minds
But never showing our thoughts on a world
That crumbles in the sublime
Poets we are, truth a delusion of sound
Speak nought those words as cold and
Bloody on sands inside
The working of words, love, pain and death
I will write poems in shallow raspy breath
Muses, quiet eyes set to disguise their cruelty
Karmic winds of my brutality
With a finger pointing at regret
Those muses I will never forget
As such inspiration in glowing eyes they set

SYMBOLIC WRATH

Would I die for the words
Only if they weren't in impurity
Be close to the words
As forth with muses I break the cold
Sullen silence
Bury me not in words
Leave it to silence
As many a poet has left this world
With symbolic wrath
Those of being truly become caught in their craft

STOP

Time trickles on with kisses of the sun
   Or trickles of rain
With sombre moments of clarity
And such calm reason that it drives you
Insane
Ahh you wonder when will it come
When heavens open up
And the starving get some
Hand on heart I have a desire
For freedom
Close to the dark
I'm left with Karmic reason
First it must be purged
Then the cessation of desire
Then we alight our nights with holy nights fire
STOP!!!

DREAM MAKER

With night bleeding not all seas are green
Purple fat delusion the puppet on the scene
Quietly with confusion I wander out
Of a dream
The maker of illusion I ponder to your
Lustful scream
The tower of the dream maker with
Lords at their rest
They squander their money whilst
I think of comfort at its best
DREAM MAKER!!!

GOLDEN MOON (SONG)

Oo Baby oo Baby why did you break it in two
Like a knife cut and cracked mirror
With bad luck that leaves me so blue

Oo Baby oo Baby why couldn't you see it through
Like a dying bird on the wing
And coldness that numbed me true

But Baby, Baby, Baby I'll hold onto you
For a while at least
Until my wits at ease
I said Baby, Baby, Baby hold onto me
Till the moon drops to its knees
And the damned scream please

Ooo Angel Ooo Angel don't leave me too fade
It's more dangerous than nightshade
Hold on Angel Hold on baby I'll see you soon
On a dew dropping moon

Ooooo Moon with a star that shines so true
No one cares and this I swear
It's in the air
Of a cold golden moon
With thieves in the shadows
And smoke in the meadows
Oo Baby, Baby, Baby

THE POETIC INTERLUDE

The night set sail and heroes began their plan
To summits of the godlike man.
With quiet pen scratching at words.
The good for thought was given to the birds

And summer shower in the quiet hour
Was warmer than I thought.
Even tho' the words were a feeling of nought
And creatures bloomed around the tomb
With wailing weeping eyes
I set myself between this world's bitter health
And made the monstrous disguise

EXPRESSION

The world ticks on with cruelty
Unkind they live with brutality
Wonders the world love does
Shows us beginning shows us above
I've stepped close to the lord's grave
Hellish they are poisoning and being poppy slaves
Not knowing the world dangles on a grave
He rose and showed me love
Not desire or hate but an expression

DREAM MAKER
OF LOVING

Water the purity of life
    With thoughts and feelings, the bloodied knife
The towers eternal in heavenly light
Become the dreams of rest on a quiet night
With my soul personified a cross we all bear
The girl is beautiful now she wont even let me stare
Too quick and nimble
With her soul at its best
I would take her in my arms and let her rest
Muses watch and Zephyr sings
The oil burning but it's not psyche this time
It's a girl of gentle wisdom in life's laughs
I would show her freedom and lay her at best
This Dream maker of loving doesn't care if she goes crazy
As the more she shines taking me for what I am

DEATH SMILES AGAIN

Dragons enslave my princess of gold
Quietly I touch Death's cold steel
Whilst Zephyr tempers my bow
Readying my arrows with a cold feel
Death smiles again knowing the guitar will wail
And Dragons feel the fear of cupids point
As Zeus folds lightning I see her face
The Dragon who thought he was a god
Is going to die and meet deaths cold steel
Those of evil will all meet the reaper
Whilst I know of the eagle the soul keeper
My hair short my curls all gone
I give Zephyr another song
Whilst he trades the devil to what he did wrong

BEGIN

With life being what it is
  The lizard died with a hiss
Sorry I am for the end of that dream
The soul scurrying into heavens light
It's knowing and sowing what's right
If regarding love you seek the scene
Remember it's golden warmth Dawn
With hope blooming in the cold disciplined morn
With time we shed our pale wanting skin
Leaving time to seek our sin
Too much too soon where to begin

RAIN

Wise you need to survive for wisdom
This unnatural disease that we call freedom
The ones ancient in its appeal
Where gangsters roam looking for power
Power you need to see the world in starlight showers
Where triads roam and soldiers belong
Fighting for freedom of rights
The eagles wing in flight
Whilst cold nurses don't really see the plight
They'd rather have affairs
I looked into the eyes of a raven golden princess
And wonder if she stared into the cold excess
The very recess of my brain unto which
I crawled back past the rain

WORLD ALIGHT

The sun is setting with the night to come
Moon is coming with stars to beset
The hot summer's night
With heavens delight
I watch with time this wondrous world
I'd set this world alight
For that very girl
But caught in another
Oh this world so cruel
I'll await, this dream maker
In passionate glance
I wonder if we'll hold each other
And take a loving stance
Penniless poor waiting for her
Gods will celebrate at my wonder
And soul dance
I might show her heaven whilst she
Becomes more studious
Yes I do love her
No matter what they say
So this poem is as strong as any
Greek play!!!!

WARMTH

Did she watch me melt
At her lustful eyes that I felt
Did she see me smile as she sung melodic tunes
Were the gifts and poetry too much too soon
She is an angel who will never die
Become my love and set to nights disguise
I will not have her scorned for her youth
Look at my words you'll see the proof
Songs sung of glory your name your very way
I would leave this town only you
Are too angelic to me, the poetic slave
The more you hide the more I feel your warmth

BENZEDRINE DREAM
(SONG)

The world we want with arising Dawn
No one knows of the earths shadows
It's set in starlight ways
Sullen puppets Unknown plays
It's quiet at night
Without the comfort
Without the light
You want to hold on tight

My heart diseased, wretched and poor
The golden warmth dying with rape
The scream primordial in every ear
Sullen puppets unknown seers
It's quiet at night
Without the comfort
Without the delight
You wanna hold on ooo out of sight

The morning never seems to come
Working speak and winsome weep
With a shinning love that's gone away
Sullen puppets and Broken laze
It's quiet at night
Without the comfort

Without you tonight
You wanna hold on for your rights
It's cold out here Dawn
It's cold out here Dawn

It's cold out here Dawn
Ooo the broken morning came
Ooo the broken morning came
I'm not blaming you
I'm not blaming you
I'm not blaming you
Oo yes I do
Oo yes I do
Oo yes I do

POETIC INTERLUDE

With hope in the morn
I'd kiss the dawn
With night on its heels
Comfort shall steal
Away our very souls
Benzedrine dream
I've lost control
Of a delightful romance
Gone is my chance
Heartbroken with the very blues
I hope to see you oh so soon

GOD'S HOLY BREATH

The war goes on, it seems as though
This world will never be at peace
The ancient ones are never easy to please
Our lives mundane death and rape
Surrounds us all
I think of the reasons simplistic views
And I am appalled
The time has come for us to unite
Be more whimsical live in childlike delight
Art is so sullen to a poet
With the shadow of death
Believing only in gods holy breath
It came to me comic yet surreal
We follow ancient ways
And thanks to gods we become ancient in ZEAL!!

DIAMOND'S EYE

The children naturally tripping
Whilst people go on slipping
Peter thieves the adults call
Their lives so refreshing
Their lives so small
Going on the strategies
We rob Peter to pay Paul
But this is not enough
With so many diamonds in the rough
But they all don't become famous
And some even become dangerous
Infamy, Villainy
Famous and Infamous
Sometimes go hand in hand
But animals we are primitive
In the Zoo keepers eye
It's not a way of living
We are all tripping in the
DIAMOND'S EYE!!!!

TRAGIC RHYME

Time fond deceiver of those
    With the broken heart
Tragedy fondness of unknown hells
But to go on we live with ourselves
Summoning spirits going with ghosts
It's not with spirituality
It's not with the host
Unknown with gods we continue
To live with time
But simplistic we live with Tragic
RHYME!!!!

TORN ROCKY PATHS

Charon calls and lightning folds
To the old gods on the lake
But seen to some the golden ones
With wine and feasts to awake
The bitter harvest in the cold moon
Will tell our stories of dying religion

But Hellhounds bay at the price we pay
For a soul and heart we shed
The kingdoms son thou knowest the holy one
Has returned for his rightful pay
It's a blessing star we watch for scars
On those we call unafraid

But hourglass and torn rocky paths
Will plague us day by day
They consecrate our malicious ways
Then say please lord let us be saved
Truly one in the glow of the sun
Will never see that day

THE DREAM OF A POET

The dream of a poet
You do but don't
Know it
The darkness cold
The flower turned
The women I know all gold
Blonde, Brunettes dusky yet
Cursed to me but I can't forget
The dream of a poet!

VIOLET LIPS

Opiates numb me
My wildest disease
Slender with hips
With rose cheeks
And violet lips
Jade in the fortune of gold
Control I had
Now I've lost my soul
He curses me with stubborn straw
Didn't he know orange means war
I'm sorry Jim!

SAD SONGS

Sad songs
For me to forget
Suicidal feelings
I hold onto regret
It's pains that come
In the motherless womb
The flowers I gave were drowned
By purity too soon

Sad songs
With wild eyes and amphetamines
I close the doors
The lights are threatening me
My timid feet are sore
Daylight robbery (They would see me dead)
Even tho' the world is a saviour
To the poems of the head

Sad songs
For this old (but young) cannabis head
Need to keep level whilst the dogs get fed
Not much time for relics lying
In my bed
I wonder if the clouds will collide
Causing lightning in the school

Sad songs
In a reaction of action with slaves
On the move
Whilst the promise of forgiven
Shall only prove
That the world belongs to the hangman
Harbinger of death the apocalyptic
Vision stolen in breath

SUMMER SHOWER

Try to tie is all I say
  Living of life it's the only way
Give me salvation
From these evil ways
True love is passion
Not a play
Stay with me it's your say
Cant resist your eyes of fire
They fill me with love and desire
Like an angel singing in a choir
Like fresh rain drops in a summer shower

DEATH OF A JESTER

Cancerous ways into your bed
Living a sweet lie inside your head
Watching waiting we all fall into line
Hidden in your heart is my time
Death of the Jester killed by the mime
Catch me running to a song
Then you'll see you were wrong
Gone the note of the dragons gong
Run out and strung and nothing left
Run out strung out you are a pest
Conscience that is

INNER SKIES

Gained so much through your eyes
People trying to tear through my disguise
Whilst I'm trying to sever all ties
And the love I was shown was all lies
Dragon of heaven fly towards my inner skies
To prove the one I love is not a lie
Even tho' a child cries

DRAGON'S EYE

Great lie I can't escape
Great love I won't forsake
Another day in the dragon's eye
Another way to tell the same lie
Shout and scream
The pain must come
Run and dream
It's the same to some
Pain and blood
On this page
Rain and flood
The unknown sage

DARK

Dark, deathly, white and shaded
The mind of the monster has not faded
It sleeps with time to think on life
It sleeps with hate and a piercing knife
It stirs in its slumber
Leaving chaos and thunder
With nothing but hate
Carved and served on a plate
Leave it all
Leave it all
Leave it all to fate

KING OF BITTER BARTER

He puts to you his ideas
He manipulates your thinking
He knows our ship is sinking
He swallows you whole
He swallows you down
He is like a revolution in a town
Who is he
He is fate
He is Karma
He ain't no fucking farmer
He has a thousand crosses
One for each martyr
He is the King of bitter Barter!

TEAR

Sane tomorrow
I could be dead
Pain is borrowed
From my head
Lessons to be learned
All in a year
Money to be earned
Gone is my fear
It now runs down my cheek
Just like a tear

SOUL

S ouls stir in the breeze
Souls turn and freeze
Without a sound
I scream and cry
Without a sound
I turn and die
Like a leave fallen to the ground
My soul speaks without a sound

TIME

Time is changing all the time
Slowly but surely we cross that line
Time is running by the hour
And it makes life taste so sour
Crossing over that line
Feels just like I've lost my mind
Watching her move from behind
Feels as tho' I've went blind
Show me a star
Show me a sign
And pray our love doesn't taste like lime
Because it's all down to time

SUNS

Turn from the sun too another light
Turn from the day too another night
With only a shred of energy left I write this
With only time to guide us we feel bliss
It's at heart our loving ways
It's a start to the precious rays
Tinkering with hate
I feel so sad
Playing with fate
I feel so glad

DESTINY

Play the tune of love
Across my heart
And the angel of love sings
In the dark
And the roses of lust grow in
The park
A devil watches for my soul
And I take absolute control
Of my destiny

UNBORN

Can't take that pillow from
Under your head
Can't you see I was almost dead
The ring of death dangling
On that thread
All in all it was all said
My heart punctured
Yet it wasn't bled

Unborn infant on a Unborn
Bed
Life and lust
My skin I must shed
All in the mind
All in the head

BITTER LIES

Got to see through bitter lies
Got to be unknown ties
She wakes with a start
And breathes a sigh
Watching as you part
And take to the unknown sky

Begin with sin it's all a game
Begin in the end we're all sane

(UNTITLED)

Fair into Life
It will never come
Fair into hope
It's a dream to some
Fair forgot heaven
My soul they sell
Fair forgot wishing
Life taught me well
Fair into Love
I need this dream
Fair into hate
It's not as bad as it seems

INSANE SUN (SONG)

Here comes the night
Heavenly and open
The bright midnight
The very witching hour

11 until 1

Then comes the day
Some say salvation
Is the only way
Hearts break and mend
The dawning hour drives you
Round the bend

Unfolding mirrors
With unknown givers
First takers then fakers
Feigning their concern

Detoxing habits that some
Live yet hate
Shows how society serves up its
Youth on a plate

Between us all the suns to blame
Giving us such beauty that it
Drives us insane

So here comes the night
The jewelled stars and cold moon
With hazes of blue which
Come too soon

Waste the dawn
Watch the sea
Become nearer to earth

And let it be

Reds and hues
I write on a purple midnight
A shimmering dawn who curses the day
We are all open to new ways

So gimme my bone
My very living way
And I'll pump and moan
Until you know what I say

Between us all the suns to blame
Giving us such beauty
That it drives us Insane
Insane sun
You are the one
Insane sun
You are the one

GIANTS

When the summer is gone and the ice the chill
Shall summon up sleeping weeping Giants
On their backs we all shall gaze
Even tho' it's loitered with shallow graves
The bones of this surrounded by muscle and vein
Grow polite foods corn and maize
The people weep at a worlds dry tear
Whilst victims and survivors cower in fear
This earth pleasurable to some
But to others it's starvation
A Buddhist blessing for my love
A head bomb that we desired for
Heartfelt I hear the whisper speak
DON'T!!!!

TURNS MY WORLD (SONG)

Trace back into time
With thoughts spilling in a quiet mind
My heart open and sore
With a beauty that I adore
Maybe she'll be my quiet loving slave
Or maybe she'll need tamed

Oh that girl
Oh that girl
Oh that girl that turns my world

Sleeping silent day but comes
I overdose on beauty you are the one
It's a world of narcotic bliss
And your heart and wickedness
It's a stolen glance but I cant persist
Town of hills skulls on dark graves
Curse this place I'm on my way

Oh that girl
Oh that girl
Oh that girl that turns my world

Well going down to the valley
With my pocket full of pills
The lizard man came

And showed me a world of chills
His echoing in my brain
Shows the girl is truly insane

Oh that girl
Oh that girl
Oh that girl that turns my world

It's insane with a broken heart

I think I'll need to watch for the dark
The girl is cold deathly and numb
I told her I'd wait till kingdom come
Yes the scaly crossed seasons
Give purity give me a reason
With open hearts and sullen ways
I didn't want to be by earths shallow grave

Oh that girl
Oh that girl
Oh that girl who turns my world
Oh that girl
Oh that girl
Oh that girl who turns my world

SEED

Got fears that will soon spread
Got pains running in my head
Darkness forms on the edge of my bed
Spreading upwards through my legs
Drinking my blood like all the dregs
Like a dog I begin to beg
With nothing left in my head
Money burns
Money is greed
Money is nothing but a seed
A deed of greed and gloom
A seed of weeds and doom

LIGHT SLEEPER

Taking a trip to the country
  Taking leave from all this chaos
Bless my legs for the long journey
Because I may not return
Heaven with me I know I wont burn
But in time I might meet the reaper
Or maybe even Satan's keeper
Bless my dreams because I'm a light sleeper

PAIN

Water so clear and pure
    Take some food and bless the poor
With a flag and a gun
We try to destroy the sun
Pain, pain, go away leave it to
The fools to pay
Help us to become
Some sort of peaceful race
We don't want to become
A rat's disgrace

HEAVEN

Greatness comes when we die
We turn the wheel then we fly
Up and up towards the sky
That must be the ultimate high
To see the colours of a dragonfly
To see heaven and breathe a sigh
Wait your turn it will come
It's waiting in the setting sun
No need to cry No need to run
Heaven is light and filled with fun

PURPLE TOWERS

I'm truly torn through lives endless ways
With opium addicts and drunken rage
I've seen some strange things
I've listened intently to the beat of angelic wings
It sounds closely to your beating heart
It leads on to things like a brand new start
My world is opening with fiction or fact
It's nothing to do with the opium withdrawn pact
I hope people change in this world of ours
And that blessings come with star glare showers
Well my coming and going in the purple towers
The princess of stars will give ambrosia for hours
It's as if I give the goddesses a gift
Be warm with passion please be shrift

STONELIKE TITANS

I had a thought that moved me
With honesty and serenity, bye bye gentle sleep
We are all arguing with ourselves
The paper folded into a gentle flower
With hurt on time
These tragic rhymes
Of broken hearts and sullen hours
Makes me wonder what happened in our great America
Fallen angels and fallen stars
The gold ness of a halo
The true cut of a scar
Are Martyrs born with souls of purity
Or do they live in the madness of soloquity
We are but bound by fate
With green envy
The cut of hate
To take what's not ours and bleed on our cross
Repenting thief
Was no loss
We are truly bound to sounds sonic waves
And found in the fortitude the captive
The dervish, lives poor ragged slave
Psychosis turning into a halo a sun
The play goes on with blessings we won
Our prophets the soap the very clean-like people
Poets have broken hearts and this should be remembered

With Dragons that were gods, turn villages to embers
We sacrifice our princess with medusa in the stars
And stone like Titans seal with concrete scars
The dragon dies at a single glance
For even heroes know you don't need a lance

KILLING TIMES
(SONG)

Time to see
Time to try
Time to watch out for the lies

No need to scream and shout
Together we'll find out what its all about
Put me in that dream around
And things will become more on the ground

Time to see
Time to try
Time to watch out for the lies

With what we've seen going around
It's with wonder we don't all run around
Sadistic and animalistic with killing
Not willing to go on living

Time to see
Time to try
Time to watch out for their lies

It was your look that set the bait on the hook
It was a book that changed my destiny
With killing times where is the
Rest of me

Time to see
Time to try
Time to watch out for their lies

DAWN TRULY DAWN

My time in your heart
It's beating and fleeting
Those eyes of desire
Sometimes cruel with the thought of school
Heavy looks with sadness
I wonder whether you care
I look for loving then see the empty stare
It's not as if I ask too much
Some warmth and care
Some gentleness
Do you know of wonderment in the summer sky
Do you see heavens in a starlight smile
I envision you in my arms with warmth on a Golden
moment
You are Dawn truly Dawn with all your golden rays
Come to loving. Come to ancient ways
Where angels beat temperate wings
Where lovers and mothers turn and sing
Hold me not in disdain
As it leaves heart shattering pain
I wonder whether you are in a thought
Of broken gentleness that you brought

ANY KIND OF ANGEL

I have hope gradually from the start
Leave me gentle sleep as I wonder if
Words will show me a way
My broken heart healing
My poetic bound words
Angels beat proudly yet never say a word
It's opium which slows the very like
My heart broken to the angel of being
This is not prose merely a seeing
The god. The wife
The heart. The struggle
The very strife
I hear a voice
It says I don't care if you die
I turn softly and begin to cry
My time will come
Tho' I fear our rape
Some unknown would surely take
I hold all honest with thunderous tears
She wont even alleviate my very fears
No wonder I'm crying when words meant nought
It wasn't her wrath that I sought
It was her eyes her smile
Her long dark hair

Now she has left me in depths of despair
Unpitious with words
As poison turns me numb
If she was any kind of angel
She would come

UNTITLED #2

I had pity once a sake that left
The cold hearted in broken morning
Disillusionment left me torn and battered
With enemies doing what they please
Turn and freeze
Souls are but food to the
Cannibals who never read
Quietly I weep
Long run short run my heart palpitates
I wonder if she'll end up with barbaric gates
Leave it all I say to wishful Karma
If they have a problem with Jim
Hold on tightly to your own sins
For redemption came in the purple skies
And Guns nor Roses will defeat his legacy

THE QUIET PEN

Flowers of aching heart with quiet disdain
The fruitful parts of Adam and Eve
Leaves us in pain
So she is gone yet here with
Quickness and icy cold tears
Words have such power in the Dawn of delight
With wondrous passion with heavenly night
The dew dropping ways of unknown fears
I live in hope!
But hope is gone to quiet golden tears
Set in the morning sun
The pen with its quiet words
Sleep with singing quiet birds

PRINCE OF TRUST

Prince of trust
Daggers of rust
So much for the kiss
So much for the buss
With quickness and coldness
Not much time for love and its goldness
It's sullen, murky, deep and converted to little sleep
With a sudden change of heart
And black minds and cold starts
She gradually moves away from me
Angelic beauty with dark hair
Doesn't even care, if I live or die
As long as she gets her fulfilment
In a world of pain Quiet I sleep with wondrous being
One godlike with crucifixions of the mind
Love her she cares little about love and it's real ways
With misfits and gone honey dewed ways

HEAVENLY EMOTIONS

Silent in the world with monstrous wound
Quiet is the girl quite mad in cold dying tomb
So with heart quiet in this world of ours
It's just a thought of loving for hours
With moderation and silent quiet slaves
We become more healthy in a world of light
Tears dawning dripping right through the night
I'm in wonderment of Delphi and Psyche
They move me so and smoulder with quiet glances
The poison I supped was but the birth of tragedy
Unknown this sickness of epic proportions
I will live with heavenly emotions

MY HEART HONEST

With slow becoming south and North
Do you really have feelings or are you cold
Winters Dawn I know you have no soul
You are gone away to the icy cold tomb
Motherless try not bearing a wound
Cold and sore with purity and heart
Hear me roar
I am shallow in breath closer to death
Dizzy in heights weighted in nights
With a worthless time
I will call on the heroes to ease my mind
Becoming afraid in this soul like tomb
He has become sullen in this wondrous room
Brooding over ancients wondering what they are saying
It was so like mystery with quiet sullen prayers
But a petition to those who are lost
Time for acquitting the very ghosts
My heart on my sleeve
Yes I was lost
In a world of disease
It's gone to the ghosts
With holy rain torn by unknown pain
That comes from literature and soaked in blood
My heart honest
Whilst tears but flood

You never know what's there in time
My world shattered by nursery grime
Its fullness
Its honest
In these words

TATTOO

It's sold gone is my lucky quiet love
Hope that's all I need
Hope the very seed
But she is a woman of quiet sullen song
With nurtured temperament
A goddess and heroine
Two
With loving shadow and old ways
You no nothing about me
Then quietly laughs
But worldly I think of you
In cold deathly gasps
I'm sorry she says
And little does she care
I want you badly
But nothing is what they dared
I did not set my heart to a sullen cold watch
I give it to thee
And you break it in touch
I do trust you
Delphi kissed my tattoo

SMOKE IN THE SHADOWS

Smoke in the shadows with fire in the room
Too much servitude in the world
We are all ragged in our own collective ways
Peace is sought by all and society a tomb
With loving ways going to a sad yet triumphant way
And hearts break every day
Crying over loss of love whilst we become a garden
unkempt
And messy in this world thinking only of our lustful carnal
sides
We escape most days into wet vibrant dreams
Not even realising that most people need warmth not lust
Saints above save me from these thoughts of total purity
As I've quit the baser matter and depravity

RAVEN GIRL

Worthless in a world and time
Well that's how I feel
I hope you know an altruistic mind
Give me both your hate and love
Live for the moment
But lover you may have
The zealot in me dancing to old ways
The people gaze on
But if you must, break my heart gently
As emotional pain is the worst type in the world
I want to show you things
Where Angels dance
And angels sing
Faeries kiss onto things
And cherubs laugh then sing
Giggling at my love plays
But tell me Raven girl
Am I your SLAVE!

THESE SAD SONGS (SONG)

Sad songs sung for tragic hearts
With melodies and new words
And feelings of blue which hold so true
We are infected with passion calmness
And trancing
Where souls dance after a fashion
The cold weariness
These sad songs
These sad songs

Sad songs sung for broken minds
The temperate beat like a heart
Which souls play on getting nearer there goals
The timing going and coming with
Slaves of blues rhyming
The words crisp and gold the words shinning
The cold weariness
These sad songs
These sad songs

Places forgotten the time gone and past
But remember those of the heart
As time of the blues comes from the start
Rhythmic pulse ignore the insults
As they come and go
And ever in the colour with mind oh so slow

The cold weariness
These sad songs

These sad songs
Are all we have
To break through pain
To face our past
These sad songs
These sad songs
Are all we have

To ease our minds
And settle broken hearts
These sad songs
These sad songs
The cold weariness
These sad songs
These sad songs

THUNDER (SONG)

I got love in my veins
I got more time than you for pain
Broken bent and torn asunder
The coming forth of quietness
The boom of thunder
My girl doesn't want to know me
Maybe she's too busy to understand
What's going on

I chant this song
Quietly
I chant this song
Finally

Well the more she breaks my heart
The more I wonder if she'll remember the start
Spoken sent and true with love
The openness of passion
Will show when push comes to shove
It's here I love
Well I don't care if she hates me
Her passion and love will save me

I chant this song
Quietly
I chant this song
Finally

Well Benzedrine pill may be
May be my thrill
But at least I don't have
A heart that leaves a chill
Blame what you want
But I have a heart and you
Broke my spirit and soul right from the start

I chant this song
Quietly
I chant this song
Finally
I chant this song
Quietly
I chant this song
Finally

ART

She cast her final spell
And I said my farewell
The life she had led she seemed
To sell
Well I hope you're right with
What you've got
And I hope you get
Get that shot
Art is born
Art is sold
Art is when I hear you man

CRY

Cry all you do is lie
Fight you know it ain't right
Run and you'll become
Another one in the sun
Blind all you can do is hide
Score from a junkies pore
Hide you'll soon see the black
Side of our love
Lead on to another love song
Head is torn to utter shreds
Bled you've just been fed
Beside a junkies open head

CHILD'S SMILE

Rivers run so very wild
Like a child who has just smiled
Mountains range so very far
Like a drunks questions at a
Downtown bar
Volcanoes erupt so very brightly
Like a dead man who looks unsightly
Cricket chirping so very quietly
Like a child's smile who has done wrong

BLOOD

Hate is underestimated
So is love
War and death lay in the
Hearts of humanity
Honour dissected
And turned to corruption
Face your fears
Before they erupt
People of the state
Are so corrupt
Drugs, guns and money
The blood of the poor they sup
Just like wine

SCARED

Paranoid people all around
    Fear filled eyes
Look to the sky
For the bomb of gloom and despair
Eager antlike people trying to get their share
Lovers walking in pairs
Psychiatrist whore peeling off those layers
A blind drunk man climbing those awful stairs
A child bent and broken feels so, so scared
(He has been labelled)

TOXIC RIVER

Like a warped stream flowing
A toxic river of the mind flowing
And never slowing until you find
That your affliction has turned
To addiction
With a needle or a gun
You find you need some
The warped stream flowing
With a lot more to come
The toxic river never slowing
It's a dark dream to some
So you've seen heaven and all is well
Too much too soon and you
Live in HELL!!!!

HUSH

Hush you can hear me cry
And it's what it seems
As you come to me in my dreams
I cry silently in the night
I know I know
You think it isn't right
But all those sighs
On my fragile soul
Prove to me I'm not in control
Of this thing called love

HEROES

The vampires move so coldly
Heroes of old move so boldly
You took the stake
And pierced my heart
And my love I did not fake
Tho' I did not move or wake
You healed my love with pity's sake
And then let me start
With a brand new beating heart
And now I pray I've hit the mark
For our souls touched briefly
Leaving each other
But never grieving
You were like a mother
Yet I went on thieving

TREES

Places like Eden on a hot summer day
The angels they feed on my loving ways
The sun so hot
The sun so bright
Shinning so lovely
On a hot summer night
With darkness to come
With it's cooling breeze
The lovers walk home
Leaving their trees

TALENT

She has a heart which beats like a drum
She has a love which will strike you dumb
She has a feel which will leave you numb
She is satin
She is silk
Her breasts are ever full of milk
Her eyes are open to the universe
She is queen of song and verse
Her mouth whispers softly unto you
She'll love you through and through
She helps you pick and choose
Her name is TALENT!!!!

AFTERWORD

Thank you for taking the time to pick up DEAD RELICS. I hope it teaches you that hope is always around the corner. We may be at war but peace reigns in everyone's heart and I hope you see the truth to the word PEACE!

CPSIA information can be obtained
at www.ICGtesting.com
Printed in the USA
LVHW110532201222
735516LV00002BA/472

9 781803 813479